S0-EWF-278

ARTHURIAN ROMANCES
Unrepresented in Malory's "Morte d'Arthur"

No. VII

Sir Gawain and the Lady of Lys

Facsimile reprint 1994
Llanerch Publishers, Felinfach.
ISBN 1 897853 34 3

Also published by Llanerch

TALIESIN POEMS
translated by Meirion Pennar, illustrated.

THE BLACK BOOK OF CARMARTHEN
translated selections by Meirion Pennar, including the Merlin verses.

SYMBOLISM OF THE CELTIC CROSS
by Derek Bryce with drawings by J. Romilly Allen and others.

ARTHUR AND THE BRITONS IN WALES AND SCOTLAND
by W. F. Skene, edited by Derek Bryce with photographs of Arthurian sites in the North.

ARTHURIAN LOCALITIES IN SCOTLAND
by J. S. Stuart Glennie.

THE MISFORTUNES OF ELPHIN
by Thomas Love Peacock. A novel of West Wales in the Dark Ages. Illustrated.

For a complete list of 100+ titles, small-press editions and facsimile reprints, write to:
LLANERCH PUBLISHERS,
Felinfach, Lampeter, Dyfed, wales. SA48 8PJ.

ARTHURIAN ROMANCES
UNREPRESENTED IN MALORY'S "MORTE D'ARTHUR"

I. **SIR GAWAIN AND THE GREEN KNIGHT.**
A Middle-English Romance retold in Modern Prose, with Introduction and Notes, by JESSIE L. WESTON. With Designs by M. M. CRAWFORD. 1898. 2s. net.

II. **TRISTAN AND ISEULT.**
Rendered into English from the German of Gottfried of Strassburg by JESSIE L. WESTON. With Designs by CAROLINE WATTS. Two vols. 1899. 4s. net.

III. **GUINGAMOR, LANVAL, TYOLET, LE BISCLAVERET.**
Four Lays rendered into English Prose from the French of Marie de France and others by JESSIE L. WESTON. With Designs by CAROLINE WATTS. 1900. 2s. net.

IV. **MORIEN.**
Translated for the first time from the original Dutch by JESSIE L. WESTON. With Frontispiece and Designed Title-Page by CAROLINE WATTS. 1901. 2s. net.

V. **LE BEAUS DESCONNUS. CLIGÈS.**
Two Old English Metrical Romances rendered into prose by JESSIE L. WESTON. With Designs by CAROLINE M. WATTS. 1902. 2s. net.

VI. **SIR GAWAIN AT THE GRAIL CASTLE.**
Three Versions from the Conte del Graal, Diu Crône, and the Prose Lancelot, by JESSIE L. WESTON. 1903. 2s. net.

VII. **SIR GAWAIN AND THE LADY OF LYS.**
Translated for the first time from Wauchier de Denain's section of the Conte del Graal by JESSIE L. WESTON. With Designs by MORRIS M. WILLIAMS. 1907. 2s. net.

Advertisement to the first edition.

But the child spake no words, but looked up at the glancing
sword blades and laughed blithely.

SIR·GAWAIN AND·THE LADY·OF·LYS

Translated by Jessie L. Weston.
Illustrated by Morris M. Williams.
Published by David Nutt at the Sign of the Phoenix 1907

Contents

	PAGE
INTRODUCTION	ix
SIR GAWAIN AND THE LADY OF LYS	1
CASTLE ORGUELLOUS	61
NOTES	99

Introduction

THE stories contained in the present volume of *Arthurian Romances* are drawn from the same collection of tales as that from which the first visit of Gawain to the Grail castle, in the preceding volume of the series, is derived. Indeed, the stories follow in close sequence, and a glance at the introductory lines of the Grail visit will show that that adventure is placed immediately after the successful termination of the expedition against Chastel Orguellous, which forms the subject of this volume. These stories practically form three separate tales, and are translated almost entirely from the same MS. as that used for the Grail visit, the fine *Perceval* codex B.N. 12576. With regard to the second adventure a few words of explanation are necessary.

The relations of Gawain with the lady of Lys, recorded in all the *Perceval-Wauchier* texts, are as a rule related twice over ; in the first instance in the section which, in my *Perceval* studies, I have called the *Brun de Branlant* section, as it is devoted to Arthur's expedition against that recalcitrant noble. Gawain's meeting with the lady takes place, as he here explains, during the siege. Later on, on the expedition against Chastel Orguellous, related in these pages, Arthur and his knights come all unwittingly to the castle of the lady's brother, Bran de Lis, and Gawain, realising the position, relates the story of the first meeting.

Now in the best and fullest texts the two versions do not agree—they are, in fact, incapable of being harmonised—and the curious point is that this second version, related by Gawain himself, and included in a collection of tales of which he is the hero, represents his conduct in a distinctly less favourable light. In the *Studies* above referred to I have entered at length into the question, and have expressed my opinion that this second form is really the older, and owes its somewhat repellent character to the fact that it is a survival of a very early, pre-chivalric stage of tradition. It is worthy of note that the subsequent

Introduction

conduct of both brother and sister is precisely the same in both versions; whether Gawain accepts favours freely proffered, or takes them by force, Bran de Lis is neither more nor less his enemy; whether she wins her heart's desire, or is the victim of *force majeure*, his sister is equally Gawain's devoted *amie*. But for purposes of translation the versions do not stand on an equal footing; and, these volumes being intended for the general public, I have preferred to follow the later and, undoubtedly, more sympathetic form.

Nor is this to take an undue liberty with the text; we are but following the example set by certain early copyists. Two MSS., B.N. 794 and British Museum Add. 36614, give the story on each occasion in an identical form. Their text, however, is on the whole far less detailed and interesting than that of B.N. 12576. I have therefore, for the terms of Gawain's recital, and for that only, adopted the version of 794; for the rest the stories are as close a rendering as may be of the text of 12576.

The first story, *Kay and the Spit*, and the taking of *Chastel Orguellous*, all part of one and the same expedition, possess a special interest for us, in that we have in our English *Gawayne and Golagros* another version of the same tales. Sir Frederick Madden, in his *Syr Gawayne*, drew attention to this, and gave a brief summary of the French text. It seemed to me that the interest of the story itself, and its connection with our vernacular literature, were sufficient to warrant a full translation being placed at the disposal of English readers. For indeed the interest of these stories is great, and if I be not mistaken, their importance as yet scarcely realised. Since the publication of the last volume of this series we have become aware of certain facts, small in themselves, but weighty in their connection and *ensemble*, which go to prove that there existed at an early date a collection of poems dealing with the feats of Gawain and his kin, which may be styled *The Geste of Syr Gawayne*, the authorship of which was ascribed to a certain Bleheris. Of this collection the story in vol. i., *Sir Gawain and the Green Knight;* the first visit of Sir Gawain to the Grail castle, in vol. vi.; and the stories here given all formed part, while our English *Gawain* poems are a late and fragmentary survival of the same collection.

Introduction

Judging also from the appearance on the scene of Gawain's son, Guinglain, and the numerous allusions in Wauchier's text to the length and importance of the *grande conte* of which these tales formed a part, it seems most probable that the original collection included a version of the adventures of the hero we know as *Sir Libeaus Desconus*, whose feats will be found recorded in vol. v. of this series. The English poem there modernised says that the hero was *begotten by a forest side*, thus apparently identifying him with the child of the picturesque adventure related in these pages. At the same time the adventures summarised by Wauchier—for he gives but little detail concerning Guinglain—do not agree with the English tradition. At a considerably later point of the collection, however, we find the young knight giving his name in terms which accord completely with our poem; on meeting his father,

>Sire, fait il, 'ie sui Giglain
>Votre fis, qui le roi Artus
>Mist nom Le Biax Desconeus.

Which may well refer to the tale we know.

This is not the place to enter into a discussion of the varying tradition connected with Sir Guinglain ; the point of interest is rather the character of the stories with which we are immediately dealing.

There can, I think, be little doubt that whoever was responsible for the *Geste of Syr Gawayne*, and whether Bleheris, whose name is more than once connected with it, composed, or merely arranged, the poems, they represent a tradition of great poetical force and vitality. The adventure with the sister of Bran de Lis is an admirable story, picturesque, vivid, and full of human interest. Our *Syr Gawayne and the Grene Knyghte* is notoriously one of the finest of our Mediæval poems. The visit of Sir Gawain to the Grail castle, related in our last volume, yields in dramatic detail and picturesque directness of narration to no other version of that mysterious story. We can well understand that, in its original form, the collection must have been one that appealed forcibly to the imagination of the hearers.

If any one will glance through these stories consecutively, he cannot fail to

Introduction

realise that the character of the hero is the same throughout. Gawain is unfailingly valiant, generous, and courteous, even, as we see in our final story, to excess. We realise as we read that, as Professor Maynadier, in his *Wife of Bath's Tale*, has well pointed out, it is in truth Gawain and not Arthur who was the typical English hero.

Is it too much to ask of the students of Malory, fascinated by the noble style in which he has clothed and disguised the real poverty of his *réchauffée*, that they should for a short time lay him aside, and turning back to the true Arthurian legend, learn at last to do justice to one of the most gracious and picturesque figures in literature—a figure to which gross injustice has been done—that, rejecting Malory's libel, they do tardy justice to our own insular hero—for not the most fanatical partisan of the Continental school has ever ventured to claim him—to the true Sir Gawain? Then, perhaps, we may have a demand for his real story, and it may be possible once more to rejoice the hearts of our English folk with a restored and modern rendering of the *Geste of Syr Gawayne*, even as Bleheris told it well nigh a thousand years ago. If that day ever come neither author nor hero will need any apology on the part of the translator!

PARIS, *February* 1907.

Sir Gawain and
the Lady of Lys

A

Sir Gawain and the Lady of Lys

HEARKEN to me and ye shall hear how the good King Arthur and his knights went forth to the wood for archery, and how at vesper-tide they gat them homeward right joyfully.

The knights rode gaily ahead, holding converse the one with the other, and behind them came the king, on a tall and prancing steed. He ware no robe of state, but a short coat, which became him right well.

Behind all his men he rode, pensive and frowning, as one lost in thought. And as he thus lagged behind Sir Gawain looked back, and saw the king riding alone and pensive, and he bade his comrades draw rein and wait for their lord. And as the king came anigh he drew his steed beside him, and stretched out his hand, laughing, and laid hold on the bridle, and said, "Sire, tell us, for the love of God, of what ye may now be thinking? Sire, your thoughts should be of naught but good, for there is no prince in this world equal to ye in valour or in honour, therefore should ye be very joyful!"

The king made answer courteously, "Fair nephew, an I may be joyful I will tell ye truly that whereon I thought. There is no king living on earth who hath had such good and such great service from his men as I; it seemeth to me now right and fitting that I should give to them that which they have deserved for the toil they have suffered for me, whereby I be come to such high estate. Fair nephew, I bethought me that my riches would avail little if through sloth I failed to reward the good service of these my knights, who have made me everywhere to be obeyed and honoured. Now without delay will I tell ye that I am minded to hold, at Pentecost, a far greater court than is my wont, and to give to each and all such gifts as shall be well pleasing to them, so that each may be glad and joyful, and ever hereafter of good will towards me."

Swiftly, and before all the others, Sir Gawain made answer, "Fair Sire, blessed be the thought into which ye have fallen, for 'tis so fair and so good that neither kaiser nor king nor count might think a better."

And the king asked, "Nephew, tell me straightway where do ye counsel that this my court be held?"

"Sire, at Carnarvon; there let all your knighthood assemble, for there is not in all your kingdom a fairer place, nor nobler halls, and it lieth in the marches of Wales, and of the land of Britain."

The king and all his company rode back joyfully, and that selfsame night did the king Arthur give command that all the knights and all the barons thoughout the land should be summoned by letter to come to him at Pentecost.

That great knighthood came thither, that famous knighthood came thither, even so have I heard, and assembled for this court at Carnarvon.

Ah God! from what far-off lands did they come. Thither were come the men of Ireland, and of Scotland, of Iceland, of Wales, and of Galvoie (a land where many a man goeth astray). From Logres they came, and from Escavalon; men of Norway, Bretons, Danes, and they of Orcanie. Never was so great a knighthood

Sir Gawain and assembled at any court as that which the good king Arthur summoned to him.

The day of the Holy Feast, when he had worn his crown at the high procession, knights and barons conducted him with joy to his palace ; and therewith Kay, the seneschal, bade them sound the trumpets and bring water. First the king washed, and thereafter sat down aloft, on the high daïs, so that all who sat there at meat might see him. Four hundred knights, save three, sat themselves down at the Round Table ; at the second were seated the thirty peers. Crowded were the ranks of the other knights who were seated throughout the hall, as was fitting, on daïs, and at tables on the ground. Then quickly Kay the seneschal bare the first meat, and the service was made throughout the hall, in joyful wise, as befitted such high festivity.

Now as the king ate, he looked towards the Round Table, even as one who would take knowledge of all, and by hap his eye fell on the seat of a knight good and true, which was void and lacking its rightful lord. Then so great a pity and tenderness took him that the tears rose from his heart to his eyes, and thence welled forth, and he sighed a great and piteous sigh when he remembered him of that knight. He took a knife which Yones held (nephew was he to king Yder, and carved before Arthur), and, frowning and thoughtful, smote the blade through the bread which lay on the board. Then he rested his head on the one hand, even as one whose thoughts are troubled by anger or grief, and unheeding, ran the palm of the other adown the sharp knife, so that he was somewhat wounded. At sight of the blood he bethought himself, and left hold of the knife and taking the napkin, wrapped it swiftly around his hand, so that they who ate in the hall below might not see. And with that he fell once more into thought and bowed down his head, and as he mused the tears came again to his eyes.

When Sir Gawain beheld this he marvelled much, and therein was he right, for to all who were in the hall it seemed but folly. Then he rose up straightway, and passed between the ranks till that he came before the daïs, and saw that the king was again lost in thought. He hasted not to speak till that he saw him raise his head, but

8   Sir Gawain and

so soon as he lifted up his face Sir Gawain
spake right courteously; "Sire, Sire, 'tis
neither right nor fitting that ye should have
such wrath or displeasure as should make
ye thus moody in the sight of so many high
and noble barons as ye may see here around
ye ; rather should their solace and their
company please and rejoice ye."

"Gawain, will ye that I tell ye whence
came the thought which has made me thus
sad and silent ?"

"Yea, Sire, that do I pray of ye."

"Fair nephew, know of a truth that I will
tell ye willingly, in the hearing of all these
good knights. My thoughts were of ye, and
of many another whom I see here, of the
wickedness of which ye are full, and of the
envy and the treason long time hid, and
now made manifest." With that the king
held his peace, and said no more.

Sir Gawain grew crimson with anger
and shame, and throughout the palace all
held their peace, for much they marvelled
that the king spake thus evilly to his nephew,
calling him in the hearing of all a traitor
proven, and all were wroth therefor.
Then he to whom the ill words were said
answered as best he might, "Sire, that was

an ugly word; for your honour bethink ye of what ye have said in the hearing of all who be here within."

"Gawain," answered the king, "'tis no empty word, thus of a truth do I repeat it, and Ywain may well take heed and know that I thought of him but now, when I sat silent and pensive, here within have I not one single comrade whom I do not accuse of treason and too great felony!"

With that I know not how many sprang to their feet, and a great clamour filled the hall. "Lords," cried Tor fis Ares, "I conjure ye by the oath which ye and I alike sware to king Arthur that ye restrain yourselves, and act as is befitting; he accuses ye all of treason—these be right evil tidings!" In like wise also spake Sir Ywain. "Ah God," quoth Sir Gawain, "with what joy was all this great court summoned and assembled, and in what grief shall it be broken up!"

The king heard, and, sighing, spake, "Gawain, I have spoken but the truth!"

"Fair Sire, for the love of God, and for honesty, tell us after what manner and in what fashion we be felon and traitorous?"

Quoth the king, "An ye will I will tell ye; now hearken. Ye know of a truth that

aforetime there reigned in this land a folk
who built castles and cities, strong towers
and fortresses, and the great Chastel Orguellous did they fortify against us. When
we heard tell thereof ye, my knights, delayed
not to go thither, not with my will! There
did I lose so many of my folk that the
thought thereof yet grieveth my heart ; the
greater part were slain, but some among
them were made captive. They took one
of my companions, three years long have
they held him in prison, and thereof have
I great grief at heart. Here within do I
see no better knight; he was beyond measure
valiant, fair of face and form, and very
wise was he in counsel. But now, when
all this great lordship was set down here to
meat, I beheld that knight's seat void and
lacking its lord, and for sorrow and grief
was my heart heavy and troubled when I
saw him not in his place in your ranks ; it
lacked but little that I were distraught.
Therefore, my lords, do I arraign ye all of
treason ; Giflet fis Do is he named that good
and gentle knight, three whole years have
gone by since he was imprisoned in that
tower, and ye be all traitors who have left
your comrade three years and have not

The Lady of Lys

sought for or freed him! Yea, and I who have blamed ye, I be even more the traitor in that I ever ware crown, or made joy, or held high feast before I knew if he might be restored to me, or where he now may be, whether dead or living! Now on this have I set my heart,—by the faith I owe to that Heavenly Lord who hath bestowed on me earthly honour, and kingdom, and lands, that for no hap that may befall me will I delay to set forth in search of him, be it in never so distant a land. For verily I tell ye all that the king who loseth so good a knight by wrongful deed or by sloth, he hath right neither to lands nor to honour, nor should he live a day longer, an he deliver not that knight who for his honour suffered toil and was made captive. In the ears of ye all do I make a vow that I will lie not more than one night in any place till that I know whether he be dead, or may be freed."

Then all cried with one voice, "Shame upon him, Sire, who will not plead guilty to this treason, for ye speak with right and reason; by over-much sloth have we delayed to ride forth and seek him far hence, even at the Chastel Orguellous."

"Lords," quoth the king, "I tell ye

here and at once that I shall set forth tomorrow, but by the faith that I owe to Saint Germain I must needs proceed with wisdom, for here is force of no avail."

"True, fair Sire," answered Sir Gawain. "Know for sooth that the roads 'twixt here and the Chastel Orguellous be passing hard and difficult; 'tis a good fifteen days ere ye be come thither; longer days have ye never ridden! 'Tis best that one tell ye the truth! And when ye be come thither, fair Sire, then shall ye have each day battle, as I know right well, one knight against the other, a hundred against a hundred, that shall ye find truly. Now take good counsel for the journey, what folk ye may best take with ye."

"Lords," said the king, "now let us to meat, and afterward will I see by aid of your counsel whom I take with me, and whom I leave to guard my land and my folk."

With that all in the palace, great and small, ate as quickly as might be; and so soon as the king saw that 'twas time and place to speak he bade remove the cloths, which they did without delay. Thereafter they brought water, and bare round the wine in cups of fine gold. Then, it seemeth

The Lady of Lys

me, there sprang to their feet at once more than three thousand knights, who cried the king mercy, and prayed that he would take them with him on this adventure, for right willingly would they go.

"Lords," quoth the king, "they whom my barons elect, those will I take, and the others shall remain to keep my kingdom in peace."

Then first, before all others, spake king Urien, a very wise knight was he. "My Lord king, ye have no need to take with ye too great a force; take with ye rather a few, but good, men, so to my thinking will ye more swiftly free Giflet, our good comrade, from his prison. Take with ye the best of your knights, 'twill be for your greater honour, and your foes will be the more speedily vanquished; knight against knight must ye fight there, and I think me that such of their men shall there be worsted that they shall that same day yield ye Giflet the good and valiant knight. Have no doubt for the when or how, but bid them make ready. I can but praise the folk who shall go with ye."

Then quoth the king, "What say ye, Lords? I await your counsel!"

King Ydier spake. "Sire, none of us should give ye praise, or speak other than the best he knoweth. Shamed be he who should give ye counsel wherein ye may find no honour. I know full well that the more part of your folk would gladly go with ye, but if ye take them, Sire, 'twill not be for your honour, but believe king Urien, for he hath given good counsel so I tell ye of a truth."

"Certes," saith Sir Gawain, "he would be false and foolish who should give other rede!" And all said, "Let it be as the king will; let him take those whom he please, and leave the others in the land."

"Ye have said well," said the king; "now go ye to your lodging, and prepare to depart, and I will cause to be made ready a pennon of silk for each of those whom I shall lead with me." As he said, so it was done, and all betook them to their lodging.

The king forthwith sent the pennons, and bade them without fail be armed and ahorse at dawn.

What more shall I tell ye? At sunrise were all the knights armed, even as the king commanded, all they who had received

tße Laby of Lys

the pennons came together ahorse before the hall.

Now will I tell ye their names: there were Sir Gawain, king Ydier, Guengasoains, Kay, and Lucans, the butler. The sixth was Tors. Then Saigremors, and Mabonagrain, who was nephew unto king Urien. Eight have I now named unto ye, counting the kinsman of king Urien. The ninth was Lancelot du Lac; the tenth Ider, son or Nut; the Laid Hardi, the eleventh; with Doon l'Aiglain have we twelve, all very courteous knights. Galegantins the Galois, and the brave Carados Briefbras, who was a right cheery comrade, made fourteen, and the fifteenth was the good Taulas de Rogemont: so many were they, nor more, nor less.

All ready armed were they before the hall the while they awaited the king, ere he came forth armed from his chamber. Then he mounted his steed, and I tell ye that, to my knowledge, was never king so richly armed afore, nor ever hereafter shall there be such. The queen bare him company even to the entrance of the palace; then she turned her back.

Then the king bade his companions

march, and they began to move as swiftly as might be on the highway, but so great a folk convoyed them that hardly might they depart or go forth from the burg. And when the king had ridden three miles he drew rein in the midst of a meadow, and there he bade farewell to his folk, who, sad and sorrowful, gat them back to the burg. And the king and his fifteen comrades rode on their way; they passed even through the land of Britain, so I think me, and hasted them much to ride quickly.

One day the king, fasting, came forth from a very great forest, on to a heath of broom; the sun was hot, and burning, and the country over large and waste. The king was so wearied by the heat, in that he rode fasting, that he had much need of rest, could he but find a fitting spot. By chance they found a great tree, where they drew bridle; beneath was a spring, and for heat and for weariness they bared their heads and their hands, and washed their faces and their mouths. I know well that one and all had much need of food, but they had naught with them, and all were sore vexed for the king, who suffered over much from the fast.

The Lady of Lys

Sir Gawain gazed into the plain, far below, 'neath the forest, and he showed unto the seneschal a house of thatch, well fenced about; "Kay," quoth he, "methinks under that roof there must be folk!"

"'Tis true," said Kay; "I will go and see if I may find victual, and ye shall await me here." With that he departed from them, and went straightway to the house; within he found an old woman, but nothing of what he sought; food was there none.

The crone spake and said, "Sir, so God help me, for twenty miles round about are naught but waste lands, know that well, save only that the king of Meliolant has built there below 'neath the trees a forest lodge. He cometh thither ofttimes privately with his hounds. There, Sir, will ye be well lodged, an ye find him; from that tree yonder may ye see the house on the hill."

The seneschal straightway went even as the crone had said, and he saw the dwelling, right well enclosed with orchards, vineyards and meadows. Ponds were there, lands, and fish-tanks, all well fenced about. In the midst was a tower; ye might ask no better, no defence was lacking to it.

B

Beholding it the seneschal stayed not, but passed the roadway, and the gate, and the chief drawbridge, and thus came to the foot of the tower. There did he dismount, but he found no living soul of whom he might ask concerning the dwelling and who might be within. Then he entered a hall, very high and long and wide. On a great hearth he saw a goodly fire alight, but he found no man save a dwarf, who was roasting a fat peacock ('twere hard to find a better!), well larded, on a spit of applewood, which the dwarf knew right well how to turn.

Kay came forward quickly, and the dwarf beheld him with evil countenance. "Dwarf," quoth the seneschal, "tell me if there be any here within save thyself?" But the wretch would not speak a word.

Kay would have slain him there and then, if he had not thought to be shamed thereby, but he knew right well that twere too great villainy.

"Miserable hunchback," quoth he, "I see none here in this house save thee and this peacock, which I will now have for my dinner; I will share it as shall seem me good."

"By the King Who lieth not," quoth the dwarf, "ye shall neither eat thereof yourself nor share it with others; I counsel you to quit this hostel, or know ye well, and without doubt, that ye shall be right shamefully thrust out!"

This vexed Kay mightily, and he sprang forward to smite him; with his foot he thrust him against the pillar of the hearth so that the stone thereof became bloody. The dwarf bled freely for the heat, and made loud lament, for he feared lest he should be slain.

Then on the left the seneschal heard a door shut-to sharply, and there came forth a knight, tall and strong, and of proud countenance, and very fair and goodly to look upon; he might not be above thirty years old. He ware a vest of new samite, furred with ermine for warmth; 'twas not long, but wide, and of ample folds. Thus was he well clad and cunningly shod; and I tell ye truly that he ware a fair girdle of golden links; no treasury hath a richer. All uncovered he came forth, in guise of a man greatly wroth, leading two greyhounds by a fair leash of silk which he held in his hand. When he saw that his dwarf bled, he spake, "Ye who be come all armed into this hall, wherefore have ye slain this my servant?"

"A curse upon such a servant," quoth Kay, "from this day on, for in all the world is there not one so evil, so small, or so misshapen!"

Then the knight answered, "By all the saints, but ye say ill, and I challenge ye for it, fair sir."

Quoth the seneschal, "Many a goodly knight have I seen, to the full as noble as ye may be, and ye be evil and vexatious, even if I have smitten this servant who roasted here this peacock, to speak thus concerning the matter."

The knight answered frankly, "Sir, ye speak not courteously, but for God's sake I would ask ye a mere nothing, even that ye vouchsafe to tell me your name."

Kay spake in great wrath, "I will tell ye willingly, so help me God I have told it ere this to five hundred knights better than ye be; know of a truth that my name is Kay."

"Certes, sir, I may well believe that ye speak truly; by your speech alone may one quickly know ye. This lad refused ye the peacock; 'tis not the custom of my house that meat be refused to any who may ask for it ; ye shall have your share of the peacock, and that right swiftly, so God help me!" With that he seized the spit, and raised it aloft, and with great strength and force smote Sir Kay therewith, so that he well nigh slew him, and know that he smote him on the neck so that he must needs fall, he had no foot so firm that it might keep him upright. And as the peacock burst asunder, the hot blood thereof ran between the links of his hauberk in such wise that Sir Kay bare the mark thereof all the days of his life. Then the knight threw the peacock to his two hounds, and spake, "Sir Kay, rise, that be your share, ye shall have no more; now get out of my sight quickly, I am over wroth when I behold ye!"

With that came quickly two sergeants, fully armed, and led the seneschal forth from the hall. He mounted his steed, and turned him back, passing the bridge and the plain, and came to where the king had dismounted.

Then his comrades asked him, "Seneschal, have ye found nothing of that which ye went to seek?"

"Not I, my lords; 'tis a right evil land here wherein to seek for food; it behoveth us to ride far, for here may we find nor hostelry, nor victual—so hath it been told to me."

Quoth Sir Gawain, laughing, "Certes, he with whom ye spake lives by meat, even as we; without meat might he not dwell in this great and well wooded land."

"By my faith, no," answered Kay, "but I tell ye truly, 'tis so proud a vassal that for naught that we may say will he give us shelter."

The king said, "Then is he right discourteous, and I counsel that we send Gawain to him. Fair nephew, go, and we will wait ye here."

Sir Gawain mounted forthwith. What more shall I tell ye save that he came straight to the dwelling, and when the knight saw him he made marvellous joy of him, and asked his name, and he answered that men called him Gawain, and straightway the knight knew him.

Then he told him his errand, saying, "The king is not far distant, and would fain lodge with ye." This was well

The Lady of Lys

pleasing to the knight, and he said, "Fair Sir, go, bring the king hither."

Then Sir Gawain rode swiftly back, and brought Arthur with him to the hostel; but ere they might enter all the waters were set free and the fountains 'gan to play. For joy and in honour of the king the knight had assembled all his folk, and received him with very great honour, and led him into the tower. The hounds were yet there, devouring the flesh of the peacock. The king looked at Taulas, and quoth, "Body of Saint Thomas, these two hounds have fared better than we to-day!" The knight heard, and laughed to himself. Kay saw that, but said naught.

From thence they passed into the hall, and when they had disarmed the meat was made ready, the knight bade bring white napkins, and pasties. After dinner he made them wash their heads, and their necks, and their feet, which were sorely bruised. Then he caused them to rest in fair beds, covered with cloth of samite, and they slept even to the morrow without stirring. But when they were awakened the host had prepared for them a right plenteous meal, this he did of his good will.

They sat them down joyfully, and were richly served. I would weary ye if I told all the dishes. The knights made much mirth of the seneschal's burn, for the dwarf would not keep the tale secret from them, but began to speak thereof. Never would it have been known through Kay, if the dwarf had not brought it to mind, for he was over bent on hiding it, and the host even more than he; all that night his comrades mocked and made sport of him even till they betook them to rest.

Next morn, without delay, the king arose at daybreak, and likewise did all the others, and armed themselves. Then the king thanked his host for the good lodging he had given them.

Why should I make long telling thereof? The king saith, "Hide not from me how ye be called."

"Sire, my name is Ydier the fair, and, Sire, this castle is mine own."

Then Ydier prayed the king that of his kindness he would take him with him, but Arthur said he might not lead with him other save those whom he had brought from his own land; and he took leave of the knight since he might no longer abide in his hostelry, and went forth with his companions.

The tale is here over long, but I will shorten it for ye. Two days did they ride without food, for they might not sooner find place where they might win food or seek lodging. Thus must they needs ride till they came to the Orchard of the Sepulchres, where adventures be found oft and perilous. There they ate with the hermits, of whom there were a hundred and more. Here 'tis not fitting to tell of the marvels of the cemetery, so diverse they be, and so great that there is no man living on earth who could think, or believe, that the tale be true. Since 'twas made and established never has the tale been told whence came those graves, nor the custom which the hermits observed; to my mind 'twould take too long did I tell it ye ere the fitting time and place be come. But this will I tell ye of a truth, when the king had sojourned two days, and beheld the Orchard, on the third, after meat, he departed, and took the road once more.

On the morrow he came to a wondrous fair land; small need to seek a richer in meadows, forests, or orchards planted with rare and diverse trees. In the forest ways the grass grew green and tall, reaching even to the horses' girths. Towards even-tide they came to a trodden way, where the tall grass was beaten to earth, and trampled down by horses, even for the length of a bowshot. "A hundred and more have passed this way," quoth the king's men.

Sir Gawain spake to the king, "Fair Sire, follow me gently with these my comrades on this wide road. I will ride on ahead, and seek out, and ask whether there be near at hand hostel where we may lodge this night, for of lodging have we great need. Yet, Sire, I pray that ye leave not the road for word of any."

With that he set spurs to his steed, and rode swiftly on his way; nor had he ridden long ere he was free of the forest, and saw before him a hill, and a company of wellnigh a hundred horsemen, who rode in knightly guise; 'twas on their track he followed.

Sir Gawain pressed on his steed, but when he had crossed the valley and mounted the hill there was never a man in sight. But he saw before him a castle; none so fair had he beheld afore, which stood on the bank of a broad river; 'twould take me over long to tell the fashion thereof, but this and no more will I say, 'twas the fairest ever seen.

Then Sir Gawain looked toward the river, and beheld two maidens, in very fair vesture of purple, bearing pitchers of fine gold, wherein they had drawn water, and he quoth, "Maidens, God save ye, and give ye good speed!" and they answered, as was fitting, "Fair sir, God bless ye!"

"Maidens, by the faith ye owe me answer me, and hide it not, what bear ye in those pitchers?"

Quoth the one, "No need have we to hide aught; 'tis but water, wherewith the good knight shall wash his hands."

"Of a faith," quoth Sir Gawain, "courteously have ye named him; great honour is there in such a name!"

The second maiden answered, "Sir, she hath spoken truth; ye will not lightly find a fairer, or a better, knight. See, but now doth he enter within his burg."

Then Sir Gawain hasted, and spake no more with the maidens, but rode over the bridge, and entered the castle by the gateway. Since the hour of his birth never had he seen one so fair, nor, I think me, so long as he live shall he see a fairer. All the way by which he passed was hung with curtains richly wrought, whereat he marvelled strangely. 'Twas closed all along with fair buildings of diverse fashions. In long rows adown the street Sir Gawain beheld rich booths of changers, wherein on many-coloured carpets were set forth vessels of gold and silver (no treasury ever held richer), cups, tankards, and dishes, the fairest ever seen, with money of all lands: esterlins, besants, deniers of Africa, and treasure trove. Every kind of money was there, and much the good knight marvelled thereat.

Stuffs there were too, of all colours, the cost whereof was past his telling. All the doors stood open; but one thing troubled Sir Gawain sore: there was never a living soul to be seen.

Then he said within himself, "Of a sooth, for love and kindness do they bear their lord, who but now hath entered the burg, company to the little castle yonder." Thus he went his way straight to that castle, and came within a goodly hall, both high and wide, and in length equal to a bowshot.

On every daïs a linen cloth was spread, and sure never king nor count might eat off fairer or better wrought. All was made ready for meat, and the bread and wine set in readiness on the tables; but never a living soul was there. In a side chamber he beheld on grails of silver more than a hundred boars' heads, with pepper beside them, dressed for the serving. Sir Gawain beheld, and crossed himself with lifted hand, but would no longer abide, finding no man with whom he might have speech.

He turned him again through the castle, thinking to find at the bridgehead the maidens of whom I told but now, whom he had left bearing the water in golden pitchers, but nowhere might he find them, and it vexed him sore that he saw them not, since he thought within himself that they would surely have told him the truth concerning their lord, whom he had seen but now enter the burg.

Much he mused thereon, repenting him that he had not longer spoken with them, but now would he make no more abiding, but set him speedily on his way, to meet the king. Nor did he draw bridle till he came unto him.

"Fair nephew," quoth Arthur, "shall we to-day find hostel where we may take rest, for we have sore need thereof?"

"Fair Sire, be at rest; food shall ye have now," answered Sir Gawain.

"'Tis a good word," quoth Kay; "right gladly will I serve the first course unto the king, and to my comrades after!"

"Kay," saith Sir Gawain "not for all the world might ye guess the marvels I have found!" Then he told unto them the adventure, even as it had fallen out, the while he guided them to the burg. As they rode adown the street the king marvelled greatly at the riches he beheld, and Kay spake a courteous word,

"Castle, he who hence might bear ye
Would do ill an he should spare ye!"

Thus came they all into the inner burg, and, still ahorse, into the great hall, but they found no man to whom they might speak, or to whose care they might give their steeds. Then they said to each other, "'Twere ill to let them fast," and the king spake, "I counsel that after supper we go forth into yonder fair meadow."

This they held for good rede, and dis-

mounted, making fast their steeds to the
stag's antlers on the wall. Then they
washed their faces and their hands in a bowl
of silver, and the king sat himself down
first, and his knights after.

With no delay Kay set the first course
before the king; 'twas a great boar's head,
and he bare it joyfully, and thereafter swiftly
served the rest, saying an any found cause
for plaint, there was no lack, he could have
at his will. "The food hath cost me
naught and I give it freely; nay, of a verity
we might, an we were so minded, feed our
steeds on boars' heads; this is no niggard
hostelry! See ye the fair couches in yonder
chamber?" And he pointed to an open
doorway.

Sir Gawain looked, and saw a shield
hanging on the wall, and within the shield
yet stood the fragment of a mighty lance,
with a silken pennon hanging from it. I
tell ye of a truth, so soon as he was ware
thereof the blood stirred in his veins; he
spake no word, but swiftly as might be he
sprang up from meat, casting aside the
knife he held, and gat him to his steed, and
girthed him tightly, and set his helmet on
his head, and sat him down again on a

bench near by the daïs, his shield beside him.

The king marvelled greatly, and the knights said the one to the other, "Ha, God, what aileth Sir Gawain?" Each would fain know wherefore he had armed himself thus swiftly; they thought of a surety his head had grown light through over much fasting and the great heat of the day. They were sore dismayed thereat, for they had seen and heard naught that might give occasion for arming, and they might not guess the cause.

The king spake simply, "Fair nephew, say, wherefore have ye ceased to eat? And wherefore thus arm in haste? Ye make us much to marvel; tell me, I pray, doth aught ail ye?"

"Naught, Sire, save that I pray ye to eat quickly, an ye love me!"

"How," quoth Arthur, "without ye, who have fasted even as we? Methinks that were ill done!"

"By God and Saint Thomas, to eat here will profit me naught; ye are wrong, Sire!" Thus answered Sir Gawain, swearing that for naught in the world would he eat in this hostelry, neither might he be joyful or

the Lady of Lys

at ease so long as they abode therein. " But I pray ye, Sire, hasten and eat."

Then the king in the hearing of all sware straitly by Him who lieth not, that he would eat naught till that he knew wherefore his nephew had thus donned his helmet.

"Sire," quoth Sir Gawain, "ill and falsely should I have wrought if for the telling of so slight a matter I should make ye fast this day; certes I will tell ye, and lie not. Ye know well how five years agone ye led an army great and strong against the city of Branlant; many a king, many a baron, with twenty thousand men all told, with ye laid siege to the city. Within were many of great valour to aid the lord who held the seignorie of that land. One morn, at break of day, they made a sortie on our host; the cry and clamour were so great that I took no leisure to arm me, but mounted my steed and rode forth, even as I was, to learn the cause of the tumult, bearing with me but shield and lance. Thus I rode forth from the camp, and came straightway on the men of the city, who were hasting to return with their spoil. I followed them, wherein I did foolishly, since I came near to lose my life thereby, for I was wounded by a spear in the shoulder, as ye know, so that I was like to die, and must needs lie sick four months and more ere that I was whole and sound.

"One morning, as I lay in my tent, I bade them raise the hangings around that I might look on the land, and I beheld one of my squires, mounted on the Gringalet, making his way from the stream where he had watered the steed. I called him, and he came to me, and I bade him without delay saddle the good horse, and he did my bidding. I clad me swiftly the while, and bade them bring me my armour secretly, and when I had armed me I mounted, and rode alone out of the camp. Fair Sire, ye followed me, ere I came beyond the tents, praying me straitly to return, but I entreated ye gently that since I had lain overlong sick ye would grant me to go forth into the fields to disport myself, and to test if I were in very truth healed of my wound, promising to return speedily to camp. By this covenant, Sire, ye granted me to ride forth.

"Thus I went my way till I came to a leafy grove, beset with flowers, and abound-

ing in birds, which sang loud and clear. I
stayed my steed to hearken, and for the
sweetness of the song my heart grew light,
and I felt nor pain nor ill. Then I set spurs
to my steed, and galloped adown the glade.
I found myself hale and strong, and feared
no longer for my wound.

"Thus I hearkened to the sweet song of
the birds till that I forgat myself, and passed
a second grove, and a third, and a fourth,
ere that I bethought me of returning. Thus
I rode till I came to a clearing fair and wide,
where I saw beside a fountain a pavilion,
richly fashioned. I rode even to the doorway, and looked within, and there on a
couch I beheld so wondrous fair a maiden
that I was abashed for her great beauty.
Sire, I dismounted, and fastened my steed
without the tent and entered and saluted
the maiden ; but, Sire, first she greeted Sir
Gawain ere that she made answer to me.

" Then I asked her wherefore she did thus,
and she answered that she held Sir Gawain
in honour above all knights, and therefore
she first gave him greeting. And when I
heard this I spake saying that I was indeed
Sir Gawain, and her most true knight, but
scarce would the maiden believe me. I

must needs unhelm, and from an inner chamber she brought forth a silken ribbon, whereon a Saracen maiden of the queen's household had wrought my semblance. And when she had looked thereon, and beheld me disarmed, and knew of a verity that I was he whom she desired, then she threw her arms around me, and kissed me more than a hundred times, saying that she was mine even as long as she might live.

"Then I took that fair gift right joyfully, and we spake together long, and had our will the one of the other. And this I tell ye that ere we parted I sware to her that other love would I never have. Then when I had armed me again, and mounted my steed, I took leave of the maid right lovingly, and turned me again for the camp, joyful of this my fair adventure.

"Thus I rode swiftly through one grove, but had gone scarce a bowshot beyond when a knight came fast behind me, marvellous well armed, and bearing a lance with a fair pennon. He cried loudly upon me, 'Traitor, ye may go no further; ye must pay dearly for my brother, whom ye slew, and for this my daughter, whom ye have now dishonoured.' Then I answered him, 'Sir Knight, ye might speak more courteously, for I have done ye neither shame nor evil; an I had, I were ready to give ye what amends might seem good to ye and to my lady; treason have I not done.'

"With that I set spurs to my steed, and he likewise, and we came fast the one against the other, and his lance was shivered on my shield, but my blade pierced him through shield and hauberk, so that he fell to the ground sore wounded. Sire, I pray ye eat, for an I tell ye more it may turn to evil." And the king quoth, "Nephew, say on speedily, and delay not."

Then spake Sir Gawain, "Sire, I left the knight lying, and went my way, but ere I had gone far I heard one cry upon me, 'Traitor, stay; ye must pay for my uncle and this my father, whom ye have wrongfully slain, and for my sister, whom ye have dishonoured!' Then I stayed my steed, and prayed him to speak more courteously, for that I was ready to make amends an I had done wrong, but that I was no traitor.

"Then we set ourselves to joust, and I tell ye, Sire, we came so hard together that we were borne both of us to the earth. Then we betook us to our swords, and dealt many a blow the one to the other; but in the end, in that I was scarce healed of my wound, he dealt me more harm than I might deal him; in this I lie not, I was well-nigh worn down, and put to the worse. Then I bethought me, Sire, and prayed him to tell me his name since I was fain to know it; and he told me he was Bran de Lis. Ider de Lis, the good and valiant, was his father, and Melians de Lis his uncle, and he said did I get the better of him, then had I slain the three best knights in any land, yet he deemed well, an God would help him, that he might even avenge the twain; for he quoth, 'I know well that a combat betwixt us may not endure over long, but that one of us must needs be slain.' And I answered, 'Sir, let us do otherwise, for an ye put me to the worse but few will believe the tale, for in this land it were not lightly held that any man may vanquish me. Methinks 'twere better that our combat be fought in the sight of many, who shall bear true witness as to the which of us comes off the better.' Thus, Sire, we made covenant together by token that in what place soever he should find me, whether armed or unarmed, there we should fight. This we sware, the one to the other. By the love I bear ye, Sire, never since that day have I heard aught of him in any land where I might be. Thus was our combat ended, as I tell ye, and of a truth I saw him no more.

"But even now, Sire, as I sat at meat, from which I arose in wrath and misease (willingly would I have eaten an I might), this is what chanced: I saw in yonder chamber the selfsame shield which Bran de Lis bare the day we did combat together; full well I remember it, and there it hangeth on the wall. Fair lord king, an God help me 'tis no lie; there in the shield standeth fast my pennon, and a great splinter of my lance; by that token, Sire, Bran de Lis doth haunt this country, since his shield be here. Therefore am I vexed and wrathful, and therefore I arose from meat, since I feared to be taken at a loss; in sooth, I somewhat fear him, for so good a knight I never saw! Sire, now have I told ye the truth, and wherefore I have donned my helmet, ye need press me no further, since not for the kingdom of Logres would I be found unarmed in such place as he may be. Fair Sire, I pray ye hasten, otherwise, an there be long abiding, I may chance to pay over dear for my meat."

Quoth the king, "Fair nephew, sit ye down again, nor have fear of any foe. He cometh not."

But Sir Gawain answered, "Sire, for naught that ye may say will I eat in this hostel!"

"So be it," quoth the king, "an ye will do naught for my prayer." With that all the others betook them to meat in good fellowship.

After no long time they beheld a little brachet, which ran out from a side chamber and came into the hall. A long leash trailed behind it, and round its neck was a collar of gold, wherein were many precious stones, red, and green as ivy leaves. The brachet was white as snow, and smoother than any ermine. I tell ye of a truth 'twas not ugly, but very fair and well shapen, and the king gazed long at it. It barked loudly at the knights on the daïs, and made small joy of them, I tell ye. Then Kay the seneschal coveted it, and spake to the king, "Sire, I will keep this brachet, and take it hence, an ye grant me this gift; 'twill be a comrade for Huden." And the king said, "Take it, seneschal, and bear it hence."

With that the brachet turned tail, and Kay with no delay sprang up and thought to seize it, but the dog would not await him, but fled on through a chamber wrought in marble, and the leash which was long fell about the feet of Kay, who would fain have caught it but might not come at it. Might he set foot on the leash he could have held it, but he failed to catch it.

Thus the chase went from chamber to chamber till five were passed, and the seneschal came into a fair garden set with olive trees and pines, wherein were more folk than in a city. They were playing at diverse games, and making such joy and festivity as 'twere overlong to recount, for that day they were keeping the feast of a saint of that land.

Beneath the shade of a laurel in the midst of an orchard a knight was disarming; tall he was and strong, valiant and proud, and to serve him and honour him the best and most renowned of the folk stood and knelt around waiting on his disarming. The brachet which Kay was chasing stayed not till it came to the knight, and took shelter betwixt his legs, barking loudly at the pursuer.

Kay stayed his steps, abashed at the sight and sound of this folk, and thought to return swiftly, and with no delay; but the knight looked on his people and said, "There is a stranger among us, whoever he may be!" Then beholding Kay, who would turn him again whence he came, he spake, "See him there, take him, and bring him hither!"

This they did swiftly, and brought Kay before him, and when the knight beheld him he said joyfully, "Sir Kay, ye are right welcome as my friend and comrade; where is the king, your master?"

"Sir, he is within, on the daïs, and with him many a valiant knight; they are even now at meat!"

"And is the king's nephew, Gawain, there? Fain would I be assured thereof." And Kay answered, "The best knight in the world is in the king's company; without him would he go nowhither!"

Now when the knight heard this he was like to fly for joy. Half armed as he was he sprang to his feet, and for very gladness stayed not to finish his disarming. A rich mantle had they hung on his shoulders, but the neck was yet unfastened, nor would he tarry to clasp it, for haste and joy. And know that one leg was still shod with iron, which hung downward, half unlaced, nor would he stay to rid himself thereof. Thus he sped in all haste to the hall, and his folk after him, and without slacking speed he ran into the hall, followed by so great a crowd that the king was sore abashed when he heard the tumult.

The knight went forward even to the daïs, and saluted the king courteously, and commanded the folk to bring torches, for 'twas scarce light therein, and they did at his pleasures, and he bade bring other meats, so that Arthur, the valiant and courteous, was well served as befitting a king.

The knight was very joyous, and quoth, "Sire, now hath God done me great honour, for never before might I do ye service; now am I right glad and joyful that ye be lodged here! I have greeted ye in all fair friendship without thought of ill, ye and this goodly company, save one whom as yet I see not!"

With that there entered men bearing torches and tapers, so that the hall, which before was dark and dim, became light and clear. The folk who had come thither that they might look upon the king, of whom they had oft heard tell, made such haste to see him that there was no space to sit down, and all the palace was but a sea of heads.

The lord was sore vexed. He held in his hand a little round staff, short and heavy, and being chafed with anger in that he saw not Sir Gawain, and knew not where he might be, began laying about him to part the crowd, making them by force to mount on the daïs, and sills of the windows, and buttresses of the walls, since he might not drive them from the hall.

When Sir Gawain saw that the folk was thus parted asunder, without delaying he mounted him on his steed. Then first the lord of the castle beheld him, and was sore vexed that he had not come upon him disarmed. Scowling for very anger, he threw his staff aside, and when he had somewhat bethought him he lifted his head, and gat him to Sir Gawain, and laid hold of his bridle, saying, "Fair sir, hearken, are ye ready to keep the covenant ye made with me? It vexeth me that ye are so far quit that I have failed to find ye disarmed, as I fain had done; I had better have been slain the day I made this compact, for then, verily, ye too had died, had I not granted the respite, but now I deem our battle shall last the longer!"

Sir Gawain straightway granted him his battle, and the knight bade bring more torches, for the stars already shone forth. Then they brought them in great plenty, and he told off folk to hold them by the fist full, so that one might see far and near, as clearly as might be. Then the lord of the castle seated himself in the midst of the hall, on a great carpet, which a squire spread swiftly at his bidding, and he bade them bring thither all that was needful to the rightful arming of a knight desirous of battle rather than of aught beside. He donned a greave of iron, and relaced that which hung loose; then he bade them bring armpieces, and he laced them on his arms, and when he had done this he came before the king and said, "Eat joyfully, and be not dismayed; behold me, that I am strong and bold, hale and swift. Your nephew on his part is even as I am; I know not if he hath told ye how the matter be come to this point that the one of us must needs die ere we be parted. 'Twere hard to think this morn that the one of us was so nigh unto his end!"

Then the king's eyes filled with tears, and the knight, beholding, spake in his pride: "Certes, Sire, I prize ye less than afore; ye are but half-hearted who are thus compassionate for naught; by all the Saints in the calendar, ye be like unto him who crieth out afore he be hurt! Never before did I set eyes on a king who wept, and knew not wherefore! By my faith, this cometh of a cowardly heart!"

He turned him again without further word, and armed him swiftly, and did on his harness, and when he was armed he mounted his steed, and bade bring a lance, stout and strong, with shining blade. Then he hung his shield on his neck by a broidered band, and settled him well in his saddle, and called unto Sir Gawain, and quoth, "Here in this house is the lordship mine by right of heritage, yet would I do no outrage nor take vantage thereof; the rather do I bid and conjure ye to take that part of the hall which seemeth best; now look well where ye will make your stand."

Sir Gawain hearkened, but stirred not, save that he drew somewhat back, and lowered his lance, and his foe, on his part, did likewise. I testify of a truth, and tell ye, that they rode over hard a joust, for as they came together at their horses' full speed the one smote the other so fiercely on the shield that both alike were split asunder, so that the sharp blade passed right through, yet they harmed not the hauberks which clung close and tight. Thus as they sped on the lances bent and brake, yet the steeds stayed not, and the knights who bestrode them were naught dismayed, but when they would have passed each other in their course they came together with such weight of body and shield, and full front of the horses, that they smote each other to the ground, and all four fell on a heap, the good steeds undermost. But the knights lightly sprang to their feet, and threw aside their lances, and drew their good swords, and dealt each the other so mighty a blow on the shining helm that it was well indented. The king and they who looked on were sore anguished and afraid, but the twain, 'twixt whom there was such enmity, ran again on each other in such fashion that, I tell ye and lie not, never was so fierce a mêlée of two knights beheld. They made sparks to spring from the helmet and smote the circlets asunder as those who make no feint to fight. When the good swords smote the shields they made the splinters to fly apace : so eager was each to put the other to the worse that they ceased not nor slackened this the first assault till that both were covered with blood. Then the heat which vexed them mightily made them perforce draw asunder, to recover breath. Too heavy and too sore had been their combat for those who loved them to behold ; never day of his life had King Arthur so feared for his nephew.

Now at the head of the master daïs was a door, opening into an inner chamber, and, as the tale telleth, in a little space there came forth a damosel, so fair of face and form that Christendom might not show her peer. She was clad in fair and fitting fashion, in a vesture richly broidered in gold, and had seen, perchance, some twenty summers. She was so fair, so tall and gracious, that no woman born might equal her, and all marvelled at her beauty.

She leant awhile on the head of the daïs, beholding the two knights, who strove hard to slay each the other. They had returned to the onslaught in such pride and wrath that verily I tell ye they might not long endure. Such blows they dealt on helm and shield with their naked blades that they made the splinters fly, and the crimson blood welled from their wounds and streamed through the mail of their hauberk down on to the pavement. Nor was the fight equal, for Sir Gawain had broken the laces of his helm, so that 'twas no longer on his head, but lay on the ground at his feet. Yet he covered himself full well with his shield, as one who was no child in sword play. But his foeman pressed him sore, and oft he smote him with hard and angry blows; Sir Gawain defended himself right valiantly, but it went too ill with him in that he had lost his helm, therefore as much as might be he held himself on the defensive. But once, as he made attack,

Bran de Lis smote him so fierce and heavy a blow at his head that, but that it fell first on the shield, it had then and there ended the matter, and all said that without fail he had been a dead man. Bran de Lis spake wrathfully, "Take this blow for mine uncle; ye shall have one anon for my father; if I may, it shall be the last!"

Sir Gawain struck back, but he was sore hindered by the blood which ran down into his eyes ('twas that which vexed him the most); he would fain have drawn him back, but Bran de Lis left him no space, so wrathfully did he run upon him, and Sir Gawain withstood him sturdily, yet so hardly was he pressed that whether he would or no he must needs yield ground.

Then the damosel of whom I spake but now turned her, and ran swiftly into the inner chamber, and in a short space came forth with a little child, whom she set upon the daïs. He wore a little coat of red samite, furred with ermine, cut to his measure; and of his age no fairer child might be seen. His face was oval and fair, his eyes bright and laughing; he was marvellous tall and strong for his age, which might not be more than four years; and by the richness of his clothing 'twas clear that there were those who held him dear.

The knights who fought below still dealt each other such mighty blows that all who beheld them had dole and wrath. I can tell ye each was weak and weary enow, but verily Sir Gawain had yielded ground somewhat, and would fain have wiped away the blood which ran adown his face and into his eyes, but he might in no wise do so, since Bran de Lis held him so close, doing what he might to slay or wound him.

Then without delay the damosel took her child, there where he stood before her, and said very softly, "Fair little son, go quickly to yonder tall knight, 'tis thine uncle, doubt it not, fall at his feet, little son, and kiss them, and pray for God's sake the life of thy father that he slay him not!"

Straightway she set him on the ground, and the child ran, and clasped his uncle by the right leg, and kissed his foot, and said, " My mother prays ye for the love of God, that ye slay not my father, fair sweet uncle ; she will die of grief an ye do ! "

Great pity fell upon the king when he

heard the child speak thus, and all who hearkened and beheld were filled with wrath and anguish. All had compassion on the child, save Bran de Lis alone, for he quoth in wrath and anger, " Get thee hence, son of a light woman ! " and he withdrew his foot so swiftly from the child's clasp that, whether he would or no, he fell, and smote face and forehead hard on the stone of the pavement, so that he grazed mouth and face, and lay senseless and bleeding on the floor.

Then King Arthur sprang from the daïs, and caught the child to him, and kissed it twenty times on face and eyes and mouth, and wept for very anger ; nor for the blood on the child's face would he cease to caress it, so great love had he towards it, for he thought of a truth that he held again Gawain, whom he now counted for lost. He quoth, "Sir Bran de Lis, this little child is very fair ; never in your life did ye do such villainy as to go near to slay so sweet a child, nor ought ye to have denied the request he made, for he asked naught outrageous. Nor will I have him slain, for he is my joy and my solace ; henceforward know well that for naught will I leave him in your care ! "

Quoth Bran de Lis, "Sire, ye are less courteous than I had heard tell, and ye make overmuch dole and plaint for the life of a single knight; ye should not so be dismayed, this is naught but feebleness of heart."

As Bran de Lis thus spake to the king Sir Gawain wiped off the blood which ran down his face, and bound up his wounds, the while he had respite; the king, who was wise enow, held his foeman the longer in speech that his nephew might be the more refreshed, for the strength and valour of that good knight doubled as midnight passed. For this was the custom of Sir Gawain: when as ever midnight had struck his strength was redoubled and he waxed in force even until noon.

Now so soon as his strength came again, and he saw the king, and his love, and the great folk who beheld them, then a mighty shame overtook him, and he ran in wrath on his foe, and assailed him straitly, but the other yielded not, crying, " Honour to ye that ye thus seek me!"

Then might ye see them smite blows great and fierce, with the swords they wielded, so that they were well nigh beaten down. Sir Bran de Lis smote a mighty blow, thinking to catch Sir Gawain on the head, but that good knight, who knew right well how to cover himself, held his shield in such wise that the stroke fell upon it, and split it adown the midst; so hard had he smitten that the blade entered even to the hilt, and his body following the blow he bent him forwards, and ere he might recover him Sir Gawain smote him full on the helm, so that the laces brake, and it flew off adown the hall, leaving the head bare. And ere Sir Bran de Lis was well aware he followed up the blow with one above the ventaille so that he bled right freely. Now were they again on a par, so that one might scarce tell the which of them had the better. In great pride and wrath they ran each on the other, so that in short space of time they had lost overmuch blood. Mightily each strove to put his foe to the worse, and all who looked upon them waxed strangely pitiful, and would fain have parted them asunder had they dared.

Now might ye have seen that gentle knight, who full oft had made offering of good deeds and alms, right well acquit himself, for so sorely he vexed his foeman that he hacked his shield all to pieces, and he might no longer hold his ground, but whether he would or no he must yield place, and wavered backward adown the hall. Then he smote him again, so that he tottered upon his feet, and Sir Gawain hasted, and threw himself upon him with such weight of body and of shield that he well nigh bare him to earth, so he drave him staggering adown the hall till he fell against a daïs.

When the damosel saw this she tare her child from the king's arms, and ran swiftly, and threw herself right valiantly betwixt the two, so that she came nigh to be cut in pieces, and cried, "Son, pray thy father that he have pity on thy mother, and stay his hand ere he slay my brother, whom I love more than mine own life!" But the child spake no word, but looked up at the glancing sword blades, and laughed blithely. And all were moved to pity and wrath who saw him anon bleeding and now laughing for very joy.

Then Sir Gawain, of right good will, drew himself aback, but he whom he had thus hard pressed drave forward at him, like one reft of his senses, and came nigh to doing him a mischief in that Sir Gawain was off his guard. Then she who held the child sprang swiftly betwixt them, and cried, "Now by God I will see the which of ye twain will slay him, for he shall be cloven asunder ere that I take him hence."

The swords clashed together aloft, but wrought no ill, for neither might come at the other for fear of the child whom they were loth to harm, and for fear of her who held him. And the child laughed gaily at the glancing swords, and stretched up his hands to his own shadow, which he saw on the shining blade, and showed it with his finger to his father when he saw it come anear, and had fain sprung up and caught the blades, sharp though they might be. And many a man wept, and there arose within the hall a great cry, as of one voice, "Good lord king, stay the fight; we will all aid thee thereto, for no man should longer suffer this!"

Then Arthur sprang up swiftly, and seized his sword and shield, and came unto the twain, and parted them asunder, whether they would or no, and said to the knight ye have heard me praise, "Sir, take the amends offered, and I tell ye truly I will add thereto, for I myself will do ye honour, and become your man, for the sake of peace." And all cried with one voice, "Sir, by God and by the True Cross, ye shall not refuse this, for the king has spoken as right valiant man." Then the knight held his hand, hearing that which pleased him.

Thus was peace made, and the battle parted asunder, and Sir Bran de Lis did right sagely, for he spake, "Sire, it were nor right nor reason that ye should become my man, hence will I do ye true homage, but for hostage will I ask the knights of the Round Table, who are the most valiant in the world; also shall your nephew do other amends, even as he promised me, in abbey and nuns, for the repose of my father's soul, and ye shall free one hundred serfs with your own hand." And the king answered, "Know of a truth that all shall be done at my charges."

Then Bran de Lis did homage to the king, and kissed him in all good faith, and then came forward Sir Gawain, and he humbled himself before him, kneeling at his feet, and praying that he would pardon his ill will; and Sir Gawain took him by the hand, and raised him up, and quoth, " I pardon thee all, and henceforth will I be your friend in all good faith and courage, nor will I fail ye for any harm ye may aforetime have done me."

Both were sore faint and feeble, and void of strength by reason of the blood they had lost, so that scarce might they stand on their feet without falling to the ground. They bare them to an inner chamber; never knight nor maiden entered within a fairer, for I tell of a truth there was no good herb in Christendom with which it was not strewn. 'Twas richly garnished, and four great tapers, cunningly placed, gave fitting light. Then leeches searched their wounds and said there was no need for dismay, for neither was wounded to the death, and within fifteen days both might well be healed, and all were joyful at the tidings.

The king and his barons abode the fifteen days at the castle of Lys, nor departed therefrom; in all the world was neither fish nor fowl, fruit nor venison, of which the king might not each day eat in plenty if he so willed. But he was loth to part from

Sir Bran de Lis, by reason of the good tales which he told concerning the folk of the Castle Orguellous, whereat the king rejoiced greatly.

"Sire," quoth Bran de Lis, "I myself will go with ye, and we will take with us squires and footmen. My pavilion is large and fair, and by faith, we will carry that too along with us; and also a pack of hounds, the best we may find, for there be thick forests all around, where we may hunt at our will, and go a-shooting too, an it please us, for we shall find great plenty of deer and other game."

Sir Gawain took little heed of all he said, so wholly was he taken up with his lady, and she forgat him not, but was ever at his service, at any hour that might please him; 'twas all gladness, and no ill thought. Nor did Sir Gawain mislike his fair son, whom he caressed right often. Fain would he have tarried long time with them. Nor marvel at that, my masters, for he was there at ease, and he who hath whatsoever he may desire doeth ill methinks to make over haste to change, nor will he make plaint, since he suffereth nor pain nor ill.

But when the fifteen days came to an

end, then did the king bid make ready, for he had no mind to tarry longer; well I know 'twas a Tuesday morn that they set them on their way, and with them went that good knight, Sir Bran de Lis.

Castle Orguellous

Castle Orguellous

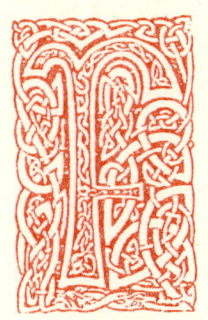

For seven full days King Arthur and his men journeyed, and passed through many a forest ere they came into the open land and saw before their eyes the rich Castle Orguellous, the which they had greatly desired to behold. They who had gone ahead had already pitched the king's pavilion in a fair meadow nigh unto a grove of branching olive trees, very fair and full of leaf. There the king, and they who were with him, dismounted gladly; they might go no further, since 'twas well known in the land that they came to make war on the castle.

They had made no long abiding when they heard a great bell toll—no man had ever heard a greater—five leagues around might the sound be heard, and all the earth trembled. Then the king asked of him who knew the customs of the castle wherefore the bell tolled thus.

Quoth Bran de Lis, "Of a truth, 'tis that all the country round may know that the castle is besieged, till that the bell be tolled nor shield nor spear may be set on the walls, the towers, or battlements." As he spake thus they saw to the right more than five thousand banners wave from the walls, the towers, and donjon, and as many shields hung forth from the battlements. Then they saw issue forth from the forest on to the plain knights mounted on palfreys and war-horses, who made their way by many roads to the castles; right gladly did the king and his comrades behold them.

I will not devise unto ye all the fashion of the castle, I must needs spend overmuch time thereon, but since the birth of Christ no man ever saw one more fairly placed, nor richer, nor better garnished with tall towers and donjon.

Now was meat made ready in the king's tent, and all sat them down to supper in right merry mood; they said among themselves that enough knights were entered into the castle to give work to each and all. Thus they spake and made sport concerning those within.

So soon as the king had sat him down Lucains the butler poured the wine into a golden cup, and spake unto the king, " I pray the right of the first joust that be ridden to-morrow morn, for it pertaineth unto mine office !" Quoth the king, " I were loth to refuse the first gift prayed of me here in this land." " 'Tis well said," quoth the lord of Lys. And the king said to the butler, " Go, eat with my nephew," and he did so right gladly.

So soon as supper was done, and they had washed, swiftly they commanded their arms to be brought, nor will I lie to ye; thereafter might ye have seen a great testing, many greaves of iron laced on, limbs outstretched, feet bent; squires were bidden don the hauberks that they might look well to them, and add straps or take away—all were fain to see that naught was lacking, but all in fair and knightly order. Ye never saw a folk thus busy themselves. They made merry with the king the while, and prayed of him in sport to say the day he would allot to each, that their pain might be the sooner ended. " Nay, lords, " quoth Arthur, " I would fain keep ye the longer in dread." Thus when they had made sport enow, and it was nightfall, they drank, and betook them to rest.

On the morrow, without delay, they arose at sunrise, and betook them to a chapel in a wood, nigh to a meadow where were buried all the good knights slain before the castle, whether strangers or men of the land. And so soon as the priest had said the Mass of the Holy Ghost, and the service was ended, they turned them again, and made ready for meat in the king's pavilion, and the king and all his knights ate together right joyfully. When they had eaten they arose, and armed Lucains the butler well and courteously. The vest he ware under his hauberk was of purple broidered with gold. Then they brought him his horse and his shield, and he mounted right glad and joyful, and they brought unto him his pennon. Thus he departed from the king and his comrades, and set spurs to his steed, and stayed not till he came unto the field of battle, whither they betook them and demanded joust of those of the castle.

Masters, at the four corners of the meadow were planted four olive trees, to show the bounds of the field, and he was held for vanquished who should first pass the boundary of the olives. Since he had come thither armed, it befell not Lucains to await long, but short space after he had entered the field he saw ride proudly forth from the castle a great knight, mounted on a roan steed, right well appointed of arms and accoutrements. He came at full speed to the meadow, and swiftly, as befitted, each lowered his lance, and set spurs to his steed, and rode the one against the other. Great blows they dealt on each other's shield, and the knight smote Lucains so fiercely that he brake his lance all to shivers, and the butler smote back in such wise that he bare him out of the saddle on to the ground. Then he took the steed, and turned him, leaving his foeman afoot, and came gladly and blithely again to the pavilion. Quoth Bran de Lis, "Certes, butler, the siege had been raised had ye brought yon knight captive, nor would ye have had further travail, for the quest on which ye came hither had been achieved, and ere nightfall Sir Giflet had been delivered up, for yonder is so good a knight they had gladly made the exchange!"

When the butler heard this he was ill-pleased, and he tarried no longer at the pavilion, but leaving the steed gat him back to the meadow, nor turned again for the king, who many a time called upon him. Then from the gateway rode forth a great knight bearing his pennon, and came spurring into the meadow, and when the butler saw him he rode against him, and smote him so fiercely on the shield that the shaft of apple-wood brake, and the knight smote him back with so strong a lance that he bare him to the ground. Lucains sprang up swiftly, and thought to take the splinters from his arm without delaying, but the knight ran upon him fiercely, and he defended himself as best he might, though wounded, but since the blade was yet in him, whether he would or no, he must needs yield himself prisoner, as one who might do no more. Thus he yielded up his sword to the knight, who led him with him to the castle, but first he drew out the blade carefully, stanching the blood, and binding up the wound.

Very wrathful was the king when he saw his butler thus led thence; then quoth Sir Gawain, "Certes, an Lucains were whole I should rejoice in that he is captive, for now will our comrade Giflet, the brave and valiant, who hath been there in durance four years, learn such tidings of us as shall make him glad and joyful. The butler is a right gallant knight, and it may chance to any that he be overthrown and wounded. I have no mind to blame him for such ill hap." Sir Bran de Lis answered, "Fair Sir, an God help me, he hath overthrown one of their men, and I know no better among their ten thousand knights." So spake Sir Bran de Lis, but for all that was he somewhat vexed concerning the butler, in that he had reproached him for not having taken the knight captive, for he thought in his heart that for these words of his, and for naught else, had Lucains been taken.

Then he came unto the king, and besought him for the great love he bare him to grant him the morrow's joust; but though he prayed him straitly the king was loth to yield, but answered that in no wise would he grant his request save that he was fain not to anger him by reason of the true faith that he bare unto him. "So God help me, fair friend; I have it in my mind that I were but ill sped did I chance to lose ye!"

"Sire, think not of that; 'tis ill done to

summon evil, an God will this shall not befall so long as I live ; doubt ye not, Sire, but grant me the fight freely, ere others ask it ! "

Then the king quoth, "Have your desire, since ye so will." With that they gat them to meat in the tent, but that day a butler was lacking to them.

Into that selfsame chamber where that good knight, Giflet fis Do, had long lain, they led Lucains prisoner, and Giflet when he beheld him failed not to know him, but sprang up, and embraced him, and asked straightway, "Tell me, gentle friend, in what land were ye made captive ? " Then Lucains told him the truth from beginning to end, how the king had set siege to the castle, and was lodged without, " And he hath sworn he will not depart hence, nor lift the siege, till that he hath freed ye." Giflet was right joyful when he heard this, and he spake again, " Sir Lucains, greatly do I desire to hear from ye tidings of the best knights in the world, even the companions of the Round Table ; 'tis over long since I saw them, or heard speak of them." And the butler made answer, " Sir, by all the Saints in the calendar, such an one is dead, such an one made captive, this and that knight are hale and whole, and to the places of the dead many a good knight and true hath been elect." And Giflet cried, "Ah, God, how minished is that goodly company; I know not the half of them who yet live!"

Quoth Lucains, "Know of a truth that all greatly desire to have ye again, nor will they know joy in their hearts till that ye be once more of their fellowship."

At these words they brought them food, and they washed, and ate, and when 'twas time they gat them to rest, and passed the night in great joy of each other's company. But the night was short, since Pentecost was past, and the feast of S. John, when the days are the longest in the year.

On the morrow the sun rose fine and fair, for the weather was calm and clear, and the king arose betimes with his comrades. First they gat them to the chapel and heard Mass, and then dinner was made ready, since to eat ere noon is healthful for the brain. The dinner was rich and plentiful, they sat them down gaily and ate with speed, they had larded venison (for of deer was there no lack), and so soon as they had dined the chamberlain armed the lord of Lys right richly, on a fair flowered carpet, and the king himself laced his helmet. Then Sir Bran de Lis mounted and hung the shield about his neck, and took his lance whereon was a pennon, and spurred straight for the meadow, which he knew full well.

Then from the gates of the castle he beheld issue forth a knight on a gallant steed, right fittingly armed, who rode at full speed to the meadow where Sir Bran de Lis awaited his coming. And so soon as each beheld the other they spurred swiftly forward, and I tell ye of a truth that they smote each other on the shield so that their lances brake, and they came together with such force that they hurled each other to the ground; but they lay not there for long, but sprang up anon, and laid to with their swords, dealing each other mighty blows on the gleaming helmets, for the worser of the twain was a gallant knight. But he of the castle was sore vexed, in that he was wounded while Bran de Lis was yet whole, and passing light on his feet, so that he pressed him sore, in so much that he might not abide in any place. By force Sir Bran de Lis brought his foeman to his knees, and ere he might rise he must perforce yield himself captive. Thus he led him to the pavilion, and made gift of him to Arthur, who received him well, and thanked the lord of Lis right heartily.

Then the king bade them make a lodge of boughs, with curtains round about, whereto they led the wounded knight to rest, for much need had he of repose. King Arthur and his men disarmed Sir Bran de Lis gaily, and he washed himself, and they made great sport all day long. And when it came to the freshness of the evening they went forth to disport themselves; many a valiant knight sat there, round about the king, in the shade of an olive tree.

Then they heard the sound of those who blew loudly on the horn and played upon the flageolet; there was no instrument befitting a watch the music of which was not to be heard within the castle, and much joy they made therein. The king was the more wakeful by night in that he took pleasure in the fair melody which the watchmen who sounded the horn made in answering the one the other.

Beside the lord of Lys sat Kay, who hearkened to the music, nor might he long keep silence, but must needs speak his mind. "Sire," quoth he, "by Saint Denis, meseemeth the joust be forgotten, for this eve none hath demanded it; the king hath neither companion nor peer who hath so far prayed it, I wot none be desirous thereof!"

"Kay," quoth the King, "I grant thee the joust."

"Sire," quoth Kay, "by Saint Martin, I were liever to handle a spit than a spear to-morrow; I thank ye for naught! Nevertheless, Sire, an such be your pleasure I will do it, by the faith I owe to my lord Sir Gawain." Then all laughed at Kay's words, and when they had made sport enow of him they gat them back to the tent.

Thus the night passed, and on the morrow at dawn, ere prime had rung, the king hearkened Mass, and when they had dined they armed the seneschal, and he mounted, and took his shield, and departed from them swiftly. No sooner had he come to the meadow when a knight, right well armed, came forth from the castle, and rode on to the field. They smote each other on the shields so that they fell to the ground, and springing up lightly they fell to with their sharp swords ; right dourly they pressed on each other, and smote sounding blows on the helms. He of the castle struck wrathfully at Kay, and the seneschal caught the blow, and the knight smote again on the boss of the shield so that the blade brake, notwithstanding he had so pressed on the seneschal that he made him by force to pass the boundary of the four olives, which stood at the corners of the field.

There the knight stayed him, and turned him back to his steed which was in the midst of the meadow, and remounted, and took Kay's horse, for he saw well 'twas a good steed, and led it away, none gainsaying him. Kay went his way back, and knew not that he had been deceived, but deemed he had won the day, though in sooth he was vanquished.

Then the knights spake unto the king, " Sire, let us go to meet Kay, and make merry over him ; 'twill be rare sport to mislead him ! " The king was right willing, so they went in company towards the seneschal,

The king went ahead, as one wise and courteous, and spake gently, " Kay, hast thou come from far ? Has mischance befallen thee ? " and Kay, who was ever sharp and ready of tongue, answered, " Sire, let me be ; ye have naught wherewith to reproach me. I have vanquished one of their knights, but he hath taken my horse ; the field is mine, for I have conquered it ; and he who hath ridden hence hath the worse ! " All held their peace, and laughed not.

"Sir, are ye in need of help ? " quoth Tor fis Ares. And then the others spake; "Seneschal, are ye wounded?" " Methinks ye limp somewhat," quoth Sir Gawain.

" Kay, hand me your shield," said Sir Ywain. " Right valiantly have ye approved yourself, marvellous were the blows I saw ye deal ! God be thanked that ye did thus well ! " With that he took the shield, and hung it around his own neck. Each joined in the sport as best he might, and Kay was right well aware thereof.

Then he spake to Sir Ywain, "Sir, I will grant ye to-morrow so much as I have won to-day, the joust and the field shall ye have in exchange for my shield which ye bear. Ye can do well, an ye will, and I were fain to repay ye in such wise as I may."

Those who heard might not refrain their mirth, and in merry mood they led him to the tent, and disarmed him, and the lord of Lys said, "Sir Kay, ye passed the boundary of the four olive trees, and he who first passes betwixt them is held for vanquished." And Kay answered, "May be, Sir, by the faith I owe the King of Heaven an ye know the differ 'twixt entry and exit 'tis more than I may do; sure, 'tis all one, for there where one cometh in the other goeth out!"

Suddenly there rang forth from the castle and the minster a peal so great and glad that ye might scarce hear God thunder, and the king asked wherefore the bells rang thus.

Then Bran de Lis spake, "I will tell ye, Sire: 'tis Saturday to-day, and now that noon be past they within will do naught against ye, come what may. In this land is the Mother of God more honoured than elsewhere in Christendom; know of a truth that ye shall presently see knights and ladies, burgesses and other folk, clad in their best, betake them to the minster; they go to hear Vespers, and do honour to Our Lady. Thus it is from noon on Saturday till Tierce on Monday, when Mass is sung, and the bells chimed throughout the burg, then they get them to their tasks again; the minstrels and other folk. I tell ye without fail till then shall no joust be ridden; to-morrow, an ye will, ye may go forth to hunt in the forest."

The king praised the custom much, and spent the night with a light heart until the morn, when he arose, and with his knights betook him to the woods, and all day long the forest rang to the sound of the huntsman's horn.

Now it chanced that Sir Gawain beheld a great stag, which two of his hounds had severed from the rest of the herd, and he followed hard after the chase till that the quarry was pulled down in a clearing. There he slew and quartered it, and gave their portion to the dogs, but would take with him naught save the back and sides. So he rode on fairly, and without annoy, the hounds running ahead, till, as he went his way, he heard nigh at hand a hawk cry loudly. Then he turned him quickly towards the sound, and came on to a wide and dusky path, and followed it speedily to a dwelling, the fairest he had found in any land wherein he had sojourned.

'Twas set in the midst of a clearing, and no wish or thought of man might devise aught that was lacking unto it. There was a fair hall and a strong tower, 'twas set round about with palisades, and there was a good drawbridge over the moat, which was wide enow, and full of running water. At the entry of the bridge was a pine-tree, and beneath, on a fair carpet, sat a knight; never had ye seen one so tall, or so proud of bearing.

Sir Gawain rode straight and fast to him, but he stirred no whit for his coming, but sat still, frowning and thoughtful. Sir Gawain marvelled at his stature, and spake very courteously, "Sir, God save ye!" But the stranger answered nor loud nor low, having no mind for speech. Thrice Sir Gawain greeted him, but he answered not, and the good knight stayed his steed full before him, but he made no semblance of seeing him.

Quoth Sir Gawain, "Ha, God, who hath made man with Thine own hand, wherefore didst Thou make this man so fair if he be deaf and dumb? So tall is he, and so well fashioned he is like unto a giant. An I had a comrade with me I would lead him hence, even unto the king; methinks he would thank me well, for he would look on him as a marvel!" And he bethought him that he would even bear the knight hence with him on his steed. Thus he laid his venison beneath a tree, and bent him downwards from his saddlebow, and took the other by the shoulders, and raised him a little.

Then the knight clapped hand to his side, but his sword was lacking, and he cried, "Who may ye be? It lacked but little and I had slain ye with my fist, since ye have snatched me from death; had I my sword here 'twere red with your blood! Get ye hence, vassal, and leave me to my death."

Then he sat him again under the tree, and fell a-musing, even as when Sir Gawain found him. And that good knight, without more ado, reloaded his venison and turned him back, leaving the knight sad and sorrowful.

Scarce had Sir Gawain ridden half a league when he saw coming towards him a maiden, fair and courteous, on a great

Norman palfrey ; nor king nor count had been better horsed. The bridle, the harness, the trappings of her steed were beyond price, nor might I tell ye how richly the maiden was clad. Her vesture was of cloth of gold, the buttons of Moorish work, wrought in silk with golden pendants. The lady smote her steed oft and again, and rode past Sir Gawain with never a word of greeting.

Sir Gawain marvelled much at her haste, and that she had failed to speak with him, and he turned him about, and rode after, crying "Stay a little, Lady!" but she answered not, but made the more haste.

Then Sir Gawain overtook her, and rode alongside, saying, "Lady, stay, and tell me whither ye be bound." Then she made answer, "Sir, for God's sake, hinder me not, for an ye do I tell ye of a truth I shall have slain the best and the fairest knight in any castle of Christendom!"

"What," quoth Sir Gawain, "have ye slain him with your own hands?"

"I, sir? God forbid, but I made covenant with him yesterday that I would be with him ere noon, and now have I failed of my compact. He awaiteth me at a tower near

F

by, mine own true love, the best knight in the world!"

"Certes, Lady, he is yet alive, of that am I true witness; 'twas but now he well nigh dealt me a buffet with his fist! Make not such haste!"

"Fair sir, are ye sure and certain?"

"Yea, Lady, but he was sore bemused."

"Then know of a truth, Sir Knight, that he may no longer be alive, and I may not tarry." With that she struck her steed and rode off apace. Sir Gawain gazed after her, and it vexed him much that he had not asked more concerning the knight, whence he came, his land and his name, but knew neither beginning nor end of his story.

Thus he went on his way, and came again to the pavilion where his companions awaited him, sore perplexed at his delay, and were right joyful when they beheld him. Then straightway he told them the adventure, even as it had chanced, and when the lord of Lys heard it he said unto the King, "Sire, the knight is the Rich Soudoier, he who maintaineth all this goodly following and seignorie; and so much doth he love the maiden whom he calleth his lady and his love, that all men say he will die an he win her not."

As he spake they beheld a great cloud of dust arise toward the forest, and there rode past so great a company of folk there cannot have been less than twenty thousand; there was left in the city not a soul who might well stir thence who went not forth of right good will toward the forest. 'Twas nigh unto nightfall ere all had entered therein.

Then the king asked whither all this folk were bound, and Bran de Lis answered, "Sire, they go to meet their lord, and to do him honour, for never before this hath he led his lady hither. I tell ye of a truth that each one of his barons will dub three new knights, to honour and pleasure him, for so have they sworn, and for that doth he owe them right good will."

What more may I tell ye? All night they held great feast through the city, with many lights in castle, tower, and hall. They blazed upon the walls, the trees, and round about the meadows, till that the great burg seemed all aflame, and all night long they heard the sound of song and loud rejoicing.

Then the king betook him to rest, and at dawn Sir Ywain prayed as gift the joust which Kay had given unto him. The king made no gainsaying, but after meat they armed their comrade well and fittingly, and he mounted quickly, and took shield and lance; nor did he long await a foe, for there rode forth from the castle one well armed, on a strong and swift steed, and spurred upon Sir Ywain. He smote him so that his lance brake, and Sir Ywain smote him again with such force that he bare him to earth ere that his lance failed. Then he rode upon him with unsheathed sword, and by weight of his steed bare him to earth when he had fain arisen, and trod him underfoot so hardly that, whether he would or no, he must needs yield. Then Sir Ywain took his pledge, and led him without more ado to the pavilion, and delivered him to the king.

Such was the day's gain, but know that 'twas one of the new made knights, not of the mesnie of the Rich Soudoier. And when he was disarmed the king spake unto him in the hearing of all his men, and said, " Fair friend, whence do ye come, and of what land may ye be ? "

Then he answered, "Sire, I am of Ireland, and son to the Count Brangelis, and ever have I served the lady of the Rich Soudoier. She bade me carve before her, and my lord for love of her yestermorn made me knight, and as guerdon for my service they granted me the joust; yet, but for my lady who prayed for me this grace, they had not given it to me, since within the walls there be many a good man and true who was sore vexed thereat."

"Friend," quoth Sir Gawain, "know ye, perchance, the which of them shall joust on the morrow?"

"Certes, Sir, I should know right well; 'tis the lord of the castle himself who shall be first on the field, and I will tell ye how I know this. 'Tis the custom therein that each morn the maidens mount the walls, and she who first beholds the armed knight take the field, 'tis her knight who shall ride forth against him. Yestereven my lady assembled all the maidens and prayed of them that they would let her alone mount the wall—thus shall the joust be as I tell ye."

Straightway Sir Gawain sprang to his feet, and went before the king, and demanded the joust, but Arthur forbade him saying, " Fair nephew, ye shall not go to-morrow, but later, ere it be my turn, 'tis for us twain to ride the last jousts ; ye shall have it when all save I have proved themselves."

" Sire, Sire, I shall be sore shamed an ye deny me this gift ; never more shall I be joyful, nor will I ride joust in this land, but will get me hence alone !"

Quoth the king, " An it be thus ye may have it." And Sir Gawain answered, " I thank ye, Sire."

Thus they passed the night, and at daybreak, when the dew lay thick upon the grass, Sir Gawain arose, and Sir Ywain with him. Know that the morning was so fine, so fair and clear, as if 'twere made to be gazed on. Then he who was no coward washed face and hands and feet in the dew, and gat him back to the pavilion. There they brought him a wadded vest, of purple, bordered with samite, and he donned it, and fastened on his armlets deftly.

And ere he was fully armed the king his uncle had risen, and they gat them to Mass, and when Mass was said, to meat.

When they had well dined they bade bring thither the armour, and Sir Gawain sat him on a rich carpet, spread on the ground in the midst of the tent, and there was never a knight but stood around uncovered, till that he had armed him at his leisure with all that pertaineth to assault and defence, so that he had naught to do save but to set forth.

Then they led unto him his steed, all covered with a rich trapping, and he mounted, and sat thereon, so goodly to look upon that never might ye hear speak of a fairer knight. Excalibur, his good sword, did King Arthur hand to him, and he girt it round him as he sat on the saddle, lightly, so that it vexed him not. Then he took shield and lance, and departed from them, making great speed for the meadow.

Now the adventure telleth that he had been there but short space when from the master tower of the castle a horn was sounded long and clear, so that for a league around the earth quivered by reason of the echo of the blast, and Sir Bran de Lis spake to the king, "Sire, in short space shall ye see the Rich Soudoier come forth armed on his steed, for they sound not the horn thus save for his arming. I know well by the long blast that he laceth on his spurs."

Then the horn sounded a second time, and he said, " By my faith, now hath he donned and laced his greaves."

For a long space there was silence, and again the horn rang forth so loudly that all the castle re-echoed, and th e lord of Lys said, " Sire, now hath he donned his hauberk and laced his helm." With that the horn sounded once again, " Now, Sire, he is mounted, and the horn will be blown no more to-day. "

This had the good knight told them truly, for the burg was all astir : he who bare lordship therein rode proudly down from the castle, and after him so many of his folk that they of the pavilion heard the sound of their tread, though they might not behold them. Even to the gate they bare him company, and as he issued forth the king's men beheld him covered with a silken robe, even to his spurs, his banner in his hand. Then they saw a great crowd mount to the battlements to watch the combat of the twain ; the walls were covered even to the gateways, so that 'twas a marvel to behold.

Thus the lord of the castle came proudly to the meadow where Sir Gawain awaited him, and when he saw him he gripped his shield tightly, and made ready for the onslaught. Then they laid their lances in rest, and shook forth their blazons, and smote their spurs into their steeds; nor did the joust fail, for they came together with such force of steed and shield and body that, an they would or no, both came to the ground in mid meadow and the good steeds fell over them. But the twain were full of valour, and arose up lightly, and drew their swords, and ran boldly on each other. Then might ye behold a dour combat, and a sight for many folk, for with great wrath they dealt each other mighty blows, so that all who beheld were astonied, and the king was in sore dread for his nephew, and they of the castle for their lord.

From either side many a prayer went up to Heaven that their champion might return safe and whole. And the twain spared not themselves, but each with shining blade smote the other, so that their strength waned apace. For know that that day there was so great a heat that never since hath the like been known, and that heat vexed and weakened them sore.

Now know ye of a certain truth that my lord Sir Gawain waxed ever in strength, doubling his force from midnight, and even till noon was past and the day waned did his strength endure, but then he somewhat weakened till 'twas midnight again. This I tell ye of a truth, 'twas early morn that they fought thus in the meadow, and greatly did this gift aid him, and great evil it wrought to the Rich Soudoier. Neither had conquered aught on the other till it waxed high noon. If the one dealt mighty blows the other knew right well how to return them with wrath and vigour; 'twas hard to say the which were the better, and all marvelled much that neither was as yet or slain or put to the worse.

'Twas the Soudoier who first gave ground; by reason of the over great heat so sore a thirst seized him that he might no longer endure the heavy blows, and well nigh fell to the earth. When Sir Gawain felt his foe thus weakening he pressed him the more, till that he staggered on his feet, and Sir Gawain ran on him with such force that both fell to the ground. But the king's nephew sprang to his feet lightly and cried, "Vassal, yield ye prisoner ere I slay ye!" but his foe was so dazed that for a space he might speak no word.

When he gat breath and speech he sighed forth, "Ah, God, who will slay me? Since she be dead I care naught for my life."

Sir Gawain wondered much what the words might mean, and he shook him by the vizor, and when he saw that he took no heed he spake again, "Sir Knight, yield to me!" And he sighed, "Suddenly was she slain who was fairest in the world; I loved her with a passing great love!"

When Sir Gawain saw that he would answer none otherwise, conjure him as he might, he cut the laces of his helmet, and saw that he lay with his eyes closed as one in a swoon; by reason of the great heat and his sore thirst he had lost all colour, and was senseless. Sir Gawain was vexed in that he might not win from him speech, neither by word nor by blow, yet was he loth to slay him; nor would he leave him lying; for he thought an he slew him he might lose all he would gain by his victory, and should he get him back to the pavilion to seek aid to bear his prisoner hence, on his return he would surely find him gone. Thus was he much perplexed in mind. Then he doffed his helm, and sat him down beside the knight, sheathing Excalibur, and taking the sword of his foe. In a short space the Soudoier came again to himself, and seeing him sit thus, asked of him his name. Then he answered straightway, and when the other knew 'twas Gawain, he said, "Sir, now know I for a certainty that ye be the best knight in the world." Then he held his peace, and spake no further, and Sir Gawain looked upon him, and said, "Fair Sir Knight, bear me no ill will for aught ye may have heard me say, but come with me, an ye will, to yonder pavilion, and we will take your pledge."

Then the Rich Soudoier answered, "I have a lady I love more than my life, and if she die then must I needs die too, so soon as I hear tell thereof. I pray ye, sir, for God's sake, for love's sake, for gentleness, for courtesy, save me my love that she die not, by covenant that, whether for right or for wrong, no man of the Castle Orguellous shall henceforth be against ye. Fair sir, an ye will do for me that which I now pray, I will pledge my faith to do all the king's will, nor shall there be therein man of arms whom I will not make swear the same. But an if my lady knew thereof, as God be my witness, she would die straightway, for never would she believe that ye had conquered me; 'tis truth I tell ye! Now of your courtesy, Sir Knight, I pray of ye this great service, that ye come back with me to the castle, that ye there do me honour, and kneeling to my lady declare ye her prisoner; an ye will thus make feint and say I have vanquished ye in fair field, then shall ye save my life, and that of my most sweet lady, and if ye will not do thus, then slay me here and now!"

Then that gentle knight, Sir Gawain, remembered him of how he had found him aforetime in the forest beneath the tower, and how the maiden who rode to keep tryst feared for his life, and he knew that he loved his lady with so great a love that he would die an she knew him to be shamed, and he thought within himself 'twas over much cruelty to slay so good a knight, and he answered. "Fair sir, certes will I go with ye to the Castle Orguellous, and there yield me captive, nor will I forbear for any doubt or misgiving. It might well turn to my shame, but even if I should die thereby, I would not, Sir Knight, that ye or your lady be wronged or aggrieved."

Then the knight spake frankly, "Sir, I am your liege man all the days of my life." And he gave him his hand, and sware straitly that he would do all the king's pleasure. And when Sir Gawain had taken his oath, straightway the two mounted their steeds and betook them to the Castle Orguellous.

Well nigh did King Arthur die of wrath when he saw his nephew ride hence, and he cried, "Now am I indeed bereft if my nephew be led therein; now will they hold him prisoner! Think ye, my lords, that he be of a truth captive?"

"Yea, Sire, of a faith, so it seemeth, yet are we greatly in marvel thereat, for we know certainly that he had vanquished and overthrown his adversary. Never so great an ill hap hath befallen any knight, for ere the knight of the castle rose we said surely that he was conquered!"

The king had no heart to hearken longer, but betook him straightway to his bed; cause enow had he for woe, or so it seemed him!

But they of the castle sped joyously to meet their lord, whom they thought to have lost, and ran to bear the tidings to the lady, who was well nigh distraught with grief, and anger, and they told her that her lord came again. " And he leadeth by the bridle, as one conquered, Sir Gawain!"

Even at these words came the knights unto the gateway, and dismounted, and Sir Gawain speedily yielded him prisoner to the maiden, saying, "Lady, take here my sword, and know of a proven truth that this good knight, your true lover, hath vanquished me by force of arms."

Never since the hour ye were born did ye see such rejoicing as the maiden made, and the Rich Soudoier spake, saying, " Ride ye to my castle of Bouvies with five hundred knights, and make ready the chambers. I will be with ye to-morrow, and would fain sojourn there ; we will have but few folk with us. Marvel not at this, for to-day have I been over much wearied."

And the maiden answered, "Ye have well said ; the castle is very fair and pleasant." With that she was mounted, and the knights set forth to convoy her to the castle. And know ye why he sent her hence? 'Twas that he might tell his men the truth of what had passed.

When the lady had departed 'twas made known throughout the castle how the matter had in very truth fallen out, and the lord bade release the son of Do, and the butler, and they did his bidding. But when Sir Gawain saw Giflet he ran towards him, and kissed him more than a hundred times, and made marvellous great joy of him. Then they sat them down on a bench, side by side, and held converse together. And when the twain who had fought were disarmed they brought for the four very fair robes of rich and royal cloth; never had ye seen such. Then the Soudoier bade saddle four steeds, and they mounted, and rode thus adown the street.

Thus they four alone took their way to the pavilion, and the king's men beheld them, even as they came forth from the castle gateway, and Sir Ywain cried, "By my faith, and no lie, I see four men come hither, and all four be knights, so it seemeth me!" And Kay answered, "I see them too!"

And when they came so near to the

pavilion that their faces might be seen, Sir Ywain ran joyfully to the king. "Sire, Sire, an God help me, here cometh Sir Gawain, and with him three others, all hand in hand: there be the son of Do, and Sir Lucains, and for the fourth a great knight!"

The king answered no word, but made semblance as if he heard not, and rose not from his couch, save that he raised himself somewhat higher thereon.

In a little space he spake to his knights, "Be not over dismayed, but make as fair a countenance as ye may; methinks they come thither to bid us return with them to prison, but I go not hence ere that I be vanquished, or have freed my comrades." And all answered, "Well spoken, Sire!"

But now had the four come so nigh that they had dismounted, and come before the king; never was seen such rejoicing as his lord made of Giflet, but now was he in sore distress, and, lo! his sorrow was turned to joy! Why should I lie to ye? The Rich Soudoier told him how Sir Gawain had conquered him, and how, by his courtesy, he had given life to him and to his fair lady;

G

and the king hearkened to the tale right willingly.

Now will I leave speaking of them, but this much will I say, that well might the lord of the castle love and cherish him who first overcame him by arms and then did him so great honour as to yield him to his lady so that his life might thereby be saved. So here will I hold my peace, no, nor speak further, save to tell ye that now was the king lord alike of the Castle Orguellous and the lands around; never in all his days did he make so great a conquest, as Bleheris doth witness to us.

Notes

PAGE 3.—*The knights rode gaily ahead.* This episode, in practically identical form, is found as the introduction to the head-cutting challenge, of which in Wauchier's compilation Carados is the hero. This double use of the same incident appears to me significant in face of the fact that the 'Carados' story is an inferior version of our '*Syr Gawayne and the Grene Knyghte.*' It seems to me most probable that our poem represents an elaborated version of an adventure which originally formed part of the compilation utilised by Wauchier in his continuation of the '*Perceval,*' and that the passage here given formed the introductory episode of the group.

PAGE 5.—*At Carnarvon.* In some of the texts Carduel is substituted for Carnarvon.

PAGE 5.—*Galvoie, a land where many a man goeth astray.* For the mysterious character attached to Galvoie (Galloway), and its connection with the Other-world, cf. '*Legend of Sir Perceval,*' pp. 186–192.

PAGE 7.—*When Sir Gawain beheld this.* There are two distinct versions of Arthur's rebuke to his knights; the one given in the text is found in B.N. 12576 (the source of this translation), B.N. 1429, Edinburgh, and Montpellier. The other version, in which Arthur refuses to explain what he means, and locks himself in his 'loge,' the door of which is broken open by his indignant knights, who insist upon knowing the reason of his accusation, is found in B.N. 12577; 794; 1453; and Mons. This latter version seems to me an unintelligent expansion of that in our text. Arthur's desire is to incite his knights to the rescue of their comrade, not to heap unnecessary insult upon them. The fact that here Ywain is specially coupled with Gawain should be noted. Ywain is one of the earliest of Arthurian heroes, appearing in the chronicles; whenever we find him in a position of importance there is at least the possibility that we are dealing with the survival of an early and genuine Arthurian tradition.

PAGE 15.—*Now will I tell ye their names.* The list of knights taking part in the expedition varies somewhat in the different texts. It is noteworthy that Lancelot is occasionally omitted, and that nowhere does he hold a prominent position. This group of stories was manifestly composed at a period when that hero was still practically unknown to Arthurian tradition.

PAGE 16.—*One day the king came forth from a very great forest.* An English version of the adventure which follows will be found in Sir Frederick Madden's '*Syr Gawayne*,' under the title of '*Kay and the Spit.*'

PAGE 25.—*The tale is here over long.* Throughout the whole section devoted by Wauchier to the *Gawain* in contradistinction to the *Perceval* adventures, there are constant references to the length and importance of the '*grand conte*' of which they formed a part. There are numerous 'Perilous Cemeteries' in Arthurian romance, *e.g.* there is one in the prose *Lancelot*, which Hector and Gawain attempt, and are worsted: another in *Perlesvaus*, and a third forms the subject of a special poem, '*L'Atre Perilleus.*' Of this last Gawain is the hero. There is a cemetery connected with the adventure of the Chapel of the Black Hand, and one in the *Queste*. It is impossible to determine the tale to which the compiler here alludes.

Notes

PAGE 28.—*Esterlins, besants,* &c. The original is *Esterlins, porpres, e besans, Deniers de muce e d'aufricains.* The correct translation is doubtful. *Porpres* is a texture, and seems to be out of place among an enumeration of coins. '*Deniers de muce*' is found in no dictionary or article on coins. *Muce* may signify *a hiding place,* hence the treasure-trove of the translation; or, as M. Paul Meyer suggests, *muce* may be an error for *murcie,* which would be the equivalent of Spanish, at that period Saracen, money. Du Cange, under the heading of '*Africanus,*' gives '*Moneta Saracenorum.*' It is noteworthy that the MSS. of later date omit these lines.

PAGE 29.—*Grails of silver.* This is the only instance I know in which the word *Grail* is used in a general sense, and it is of value as indicating the meaning which the writers of that period attached to the word.

PAGE 38.—*Ider de Lis.* The father's name is more generally given as Norres de Lis. Llys is the Welsh for castle, and the spelling of the word varies in the texts. Brandelis is, as a rule, written in one word, and spelt with an *i*; when the castle alone is spoken of it is written Lys. I have endeavoured to indicate this peculiarity in the translation. Cf. Gawain's appeal to his uncle to eat, and Arthur's refusal, with *Arthur* and *Gorlagon* published by Prof. Kittredge; cf. *Folk-Lore,* March 1904, where a translation of this curious tale, with explanatory comment, is given.

PAGE 41.—*A comrade for Huden.* Huden, or Hudenc, is Tristan's dog. The reference is interesting, as showing a knowledge of the *Tristan* story on the part of the compiler. That hero, however, plays no part in this group of tales.

PAGE 48.—*There came forth a damosel.* The lady's name is not given here, but later on she is called Guilorete, and in other texts Gloriete.

II

PAGE 63.—*Castle Orguellous.* This adventure, under the title of '*Gawain and Golagros,*' will be found in Madden's '*Syr Gawayne,*' but the version is much condensed. In the English poem Espinogres plays the *rôle* here assigned to Bran de Lis, and explains the customs of the castle.

PAGE 70.—'*Tis ill done to summon evil.* The original gives '*On ne doit pas mal senechier.*' This latter word appears to be unknown. I submitted the passage to M. Paul Meyer, who thinks it may be a fault of the copyist; at the same time, Godefroi gives the noun *senechiance* as equivalent to *segnefiance*, and a verb may have been constructed from this. The corresponding passage in B. N. 12577 runs '*Nul ne doit le mal prononcier.*' In an article in *Folk Lore* for March 1907, Miss Goodrich Freer quotes a Gaelic proverb, 'Ill will come if mentioned.' This seems to be the equivalent of our text.

PAGE 87.—*A horn was sounded.* In the English version a small bell is rung. Much less stress is laid upon the arming of the knight, which here is a most picturesque and effective passage.

PAGE 93.—*When that gentle knight Sir Gawain.* Gawain's extreme courtesy, and the consequent dismay of the king, are related in much the same terms, but more condensed, in the English poem. It seems possible that it was this adventure of the Rich Soudoier which suggested the figure of Galehault, '*le haut prince*' in the prose Lancelot. Both are distinguished for their height, their beauty, and their opposition to Arthur. Both, alike, became the King's friends through the courtesy and feigned submission of the knights Gawain and Lancelot. The parallel is worth working out.

PAGE 98.—*As Bleheris doth witness to us.* Other forms of the name are Bleobleheris (B.N. 1453) and Bliobliheri

(B.N. Add. 36614). This latter MS. at a later stage of the same collection again cites Bleheris as authority for the story of Gawain and the magic shield ; he is there said to have been born and brought up in Wales. He is probably identical with the Bledhericus mentioned by Giraldus Cambrensis as a famous story teller, *famosus ille fabulator.* For a full discussion of the whole question see my *Legend of Sir Perceval.*